THE TRAIN NOW STANDING

Volume One

Life and Times of the Hull and Barnsley Railway:

A Pictorial Miscellany

compiled by

Ted Dodsworth

HUTTON PRESS

1990

Published by the Hutton Press Ltd
130 Canada Drive, Cherry Burton, Beverley
East Yorkshire HU17 7SB

Copyright © 1990
Published 1990
Reprinted 1996

Printed and bound by Clifford Ward & Co. (Bridlington) Ltd
55 West Street, Bridlington, East Yorkshire
YO15 3DZ

ISBN 0 907033 95 4

DEDICATION

To the memory of the men and women,
servants of the Hull & Barnsley Railway.

ACKNOWLEDGEMENTS

The author is indebted to the many individuals and organisations without whose assistance this volume would not have been possible. Particular thanks go to the following: the administrators and staffs of Hull Local Studies Library, the Hull City Records Office, the Hull Town Docks Museum and the Hull Transport Museum, the Hull & Barnsley Stock Fund and their Publicity Officer Martin Barker, Peter Longhorn, Walter Oglesby, Peter Wilkes, Eric Cracknell, Alan Beacock, Harry Jordan, Ideal Standard Ltd., Christopher Ketchell, Brian Latus, C. and L. Collingwood, Joyce and Christopher Young, Eddie Holland, Derek Vine, Ian Scotney, L. S. R. Baker, Phil Hickson, Ted Tuxworth, Arthur Stephenson, Mrs. E. Glen and Tom Makey.

INTRODUCTION

Continuing to illustrate the development of transport in the Hull & Yorkshire district, the author has chosen to follow his previous successful titles, in which he describes early methods of road transport and pioneer aviation in the region, with a volume dedicated to the life and times of the Hull & Barnsley Railway. Commencing at the Company's Alexandra Dock, Hull, and terminating at the Midland Railway Company's Cudworth Station, the author, using a wealth of photographic material from his collection and other sources, has chronicled various aspects of the Railway, including some of its day to day activities, mostly in the period before the line was amalgamated with the North Eastern Railway in 1922. As well as the daily routine the author has highlighted people and places of interest along the route of what was to be one of the last great promotions of the 19th century, the Hull & Barnsley Railway.

PREFACE

The origins of the Railway can be traced to the 1870-1880 period when an upsurge in trade stretched to breaking point the antiquated port facilities at the Hull docks. In an attempt to ease the situation the North Eastern Railway, which had the monopoly of the rail routes into Hull, began to divert traffic to the ports of Hartlepool, Goole and Grimsby. Local business interests, outraged by this turn of events, reacted by calling for the establishment of a railway system independent of the North Eastern. In 1879, following the meeting of an influential group of merchants, bankers and ship owners, the formation of the Hull, Barnsley & West Riding Junction Railway & Dock Company was announced. The scheme was to include a new deep water dock. The following year plans for the new Railway were laid before Parliament. The Hull Corporation agreed to sell to the Railway Company 126 acres of land on the site of what was eventually to become Alexandra Dock. Although the North Eastern Railway Company energetically opposed the HB&WRJR&DCo.'s petition the Act received the Royal Assent in August 1880. January 15th 1881 witnessed the ceremony of the cutting of the first sod of earth, by the Chairman, Gerard Smith, on the site of the Company's new dock. During the construction of the Railway costs escalated far beyond the original design estimates. Due to the nature of Hull's subsoil and the hard chalk rock encountered on sections of the route, progress was slow and laborious, explosive charges being resorted to at Drewton Cutting and Tunnel. Other items which had cost more than expected were stations and land purchases. By the middle of 1884, as a result of the Company's inability to pay the contractors constructing the railway, work was suspended. Later in the year work resumed after a further injection of capital, raised from an issue of shares sanctioned by Parliament. The last promotion of a major new railway company in the 19th century, the Hull & Barnsley project, at a cost of almost £6 million, was finally completed and opened for traffic in July 1885.

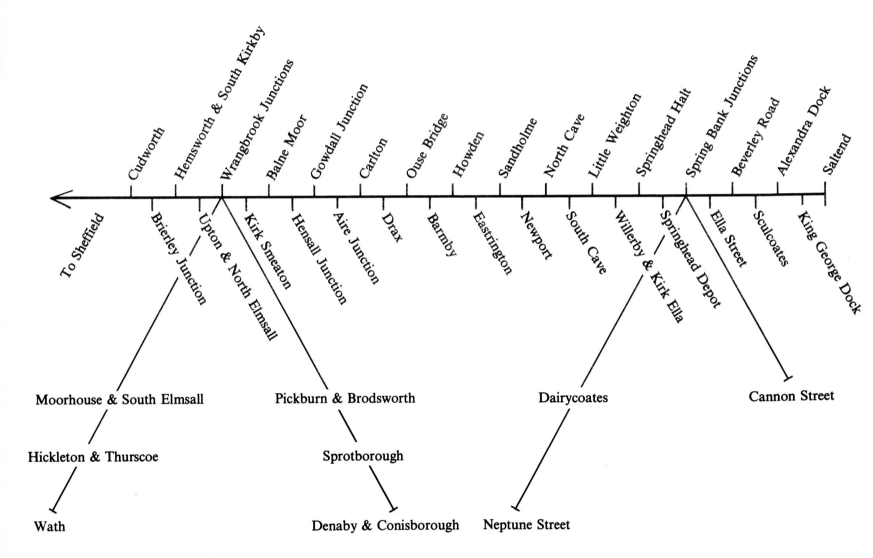

Cudworth
Hemsworth & South Kirkby
Wrangbrook Junctions
Balne Moor
Gowdall Junction
Carlton
Ouse Bridge
Howden
Sandholme
North Cave
Little Weighton
Springhead Halt
Spring Bank Junctions
Beverley Road
Alexandra Dock
Saltend

To Sheffield
Brierley Junction
Upton & North Elmsall
Kirk Smeaton
Hensall Junction
Aire Junction
Drax
Barmby
Eastrington
Newport
South Cave
Willerby & Kirk Ella
Springhead Depot
Ella Street
Sculcoates
King George Dock

Moorhouse & South Elmsall
Pickburn & Brodsworth
Dairycoates
Cannon Street

Hickleton & Thurscoe
Sprotborough

Wath
Denaby & Conisborough
Neptune Street

6

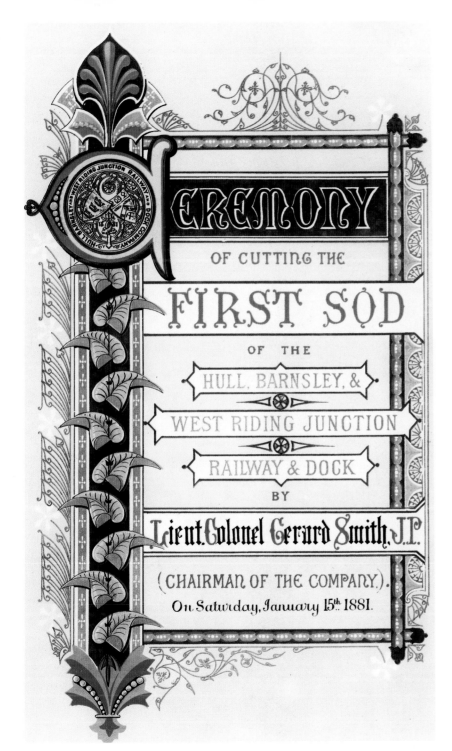

CEREMONY

OF CUTTING THE

FIRST SOD

OF THE

HULL, BARNSLEY, &

WEST RIDING JUNCTION

RAILWAY & DOCK

BY

Lieut. Colonel Gerard Smith, J.P.

(CHAIRMAN OF THE COMPANY.)

On Saturday, January 15th 1881.

Vote for

Yours Faithfully
Gerard Smith

Descended from an old established Hull banking family, Gerard Smith was to become the first chairman of the Hull, Barnsley, & West Riding Junction Railway & Dock Co. Illustration reproduced from an electioneering Handbill. Colonel Smith was elected Member of Parliament for High Wycombe in 1883.

The superbly illuminated cover of the programme to commemorate the cutting of the first sod of the future Alexandra Dock in 1881. Lieutenant Colonel Gerard Smith, J.P., Chairman of the Company, officiated at the occasion. The day was bleak and bitterly cold, snow covered the ground and the cutting ceremony took place in a snowstorm. The day was declared a public holiday with many thousands witnessing the public processions and cutting ceremony.

Illustration reproduced by kind permission of the Hull Transport Museum.

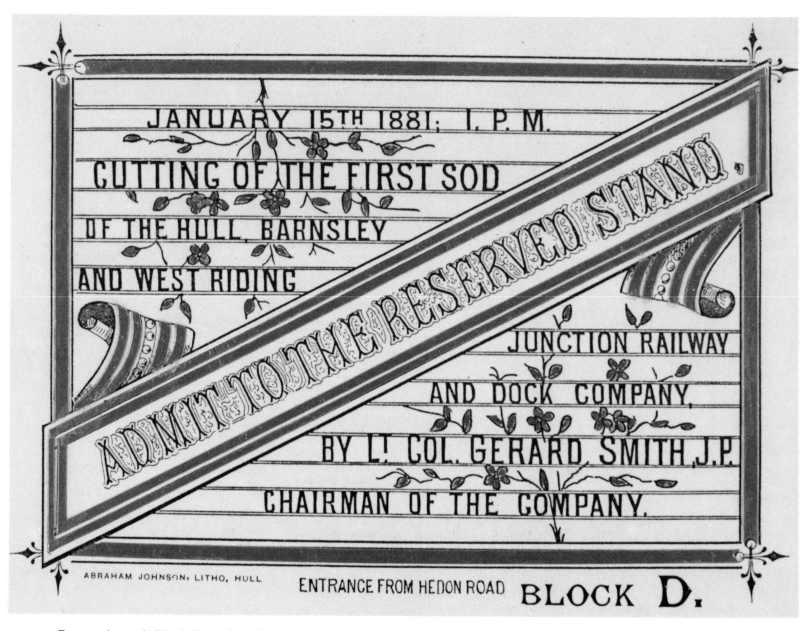

Reserved stand, Block D, white colour ticket permitted the holder to witness the ceremony of cutting the first sod at the Hull & Barnsley Railway's Alexandra Dock, January 15th, 1881.
Illustration courtesy of Hull Local Studies Library, Humberside Leisure Services.

ALEXANDRA DOCK

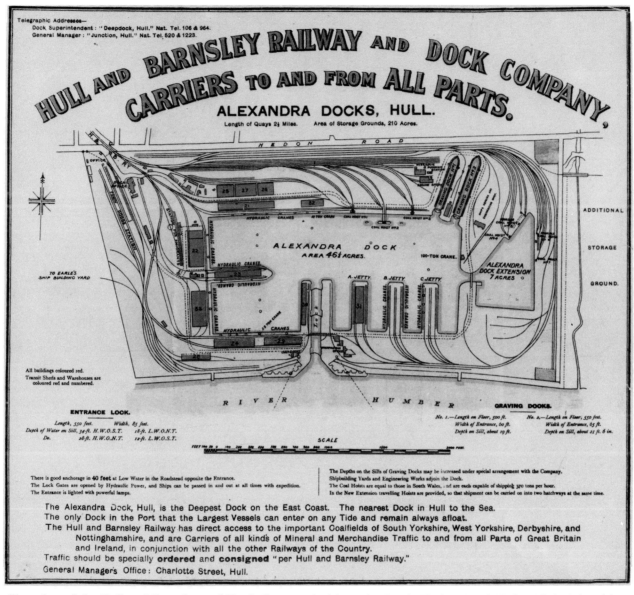

Plan view of the Hull and Barnsley and Dock Company's Alexandra Dock, Hedon Road, Hull, c.1910. Advertising material such as this was distributed to agents of the Company and to offices throughout the Railway's system. The new dock, named Alexandra after the Princess of Wales, was opened by Mrs Smith, wife of the Chairman of the Company Lt-Col. Gerard Smith. It was hoped that the Prince and Princess of Wales would attend the ceremony but they were unable to accept the invitation.

continued on Page 12

'INVISIBLE GREEN'

6 COUPLED TANK ENGINE, HULL & BARNSLEY RLY.

Five 0-6-2T tank engines were ordered by the Lancashire, Derbyshire & East Coast Railway in 1900. Of these only one was delivered. Because of financial difficulties this was returned to the manufacturers, Kitson & Company, and the balance cancelled. The original order of five was offered to, and taken up by, the Hull & Barnsley Railway. Delivery commenced in January 1901 and was completed in the following month. Ordered by the LD&ECR as Class A, the H&B accorded the 0-6-2Ts the classification F1 in 1908.

The appointment of Matthew Stirling as Locomotive Superintendent brought about subtle changes to the lined black locomotive livery originally adopted by William Kirtley during his brief period of consultancy. Although Stirling's colour scheme resembled Kirtley's original, a distinct translucent green was visible in the black paintwork when viewed in strong light. To achieve this effect a process of mixing equal proportions of 'drop black' and Brunswick green created a finish known as 'invisible green'. Lining consisted of broad bands of ultramarine finished with fine vermillion lines on each edge. The accompanying colour illustrations from the period give a good indication of the livery adopted by Matthew Stirling.

'Black Looks'. Superb colour reproduction issued in 1907 to coincide with the introduction of the Hull & Barnsley's Class A mineral engine. The 0-8-0 heavyweight is portrayed by the popular Edwardian railway illustrator, F. Moore. It is believed that the prolific amount of material issued in the name of this specialist may have come from a school of artists producing work under the pseudonym of Moore.

'Black and Blue'. Reproduced from a contemporary colour print, the handsome outline of the Hull & Barnsley passenger express locomotive is enhanced by a balanced colour combination of black paintwork, relieved by broad blue lining. Gold lettering and vermillion detailing contribute to complete the overall effect. Visible on the original artwork, the Class J's boiler displays a hint of 'invisible green'. Emblazoned on the leading splasher, the Hull & Barnsley armorial device (a slightly modified design from that featured on the front cover) was exclusive to this class of engine.

'Discharging Pit Props, Alexandra Dock, Hull'. Official Hull & Barnsley postcard view of pit props being unloaded at the Company's Alexandra Dock. An impression of the huge quantities of timber imports can be gauged from the amounts of pit props stacked on the dockside and loaded in returning mineral wagons. Pyman, Bell & Co were the port's major importer of pit props and largest customers of the Hull & Barnsley for mining timber.

'Coal awaiting shipment, at Alexandra Docks, Hull'. At its peak in 1913 the Hull & Barnsley Dock handled almost 3 million tons of coal. The volume of export coal traffic passing through the Alexandra Docks can be judged from this official postcard view of hundreds of wagon loads waiting for shipment. Noted amongst the multitude of private owner wagons are coal trucks of the Great Central Railway.

TIMBER TRADE

Alexandra Dock side, timber train, c.1906. Recently discharged deals of timber roped on to Hull & Barnsley timber bogies are pictured waiting to be shunted through the dock's rail network before being deposited on the many acres of storage land adjoining the busy dock. Also observed is Hull carting agent, J. C. Robinson, making a collection of imported pork produce.

Throughout its existence, the Hull & Barnsley Railway did not operate its own cartage vehicles. Instead the Company was content to employ the services of Greenwood Brothers, general carriers and carting agents, and Suttons parcel carriers.

Stacking timber, Horsley's wood yard, Alexandra Dock, c.1902. Sawn wood and general timber were valuable imports to the Hull & Barnsley, a brisk trade having been built up with continental ports.

TIMBER LINE

Bird's-eye view of vast quantities of timber stacked in open storage at the Hull & Barnsley's Alexandra Dock riverside wood yards. An indication of the large amounts of imported sawn wood and pit props then handled by the Company can be seen from this 1920s photograph of the dock's timber yards packed to near capacity. Timber vessels are pictured moored throughout the wood yard area, and two ships tied up in the foreground of the illustration are secured in the waters of the dock's later 7 acre development.

FIRST IN LINE

Sawn timber stacks, Alexandra Dock, c.1910. George Horsley & Co., one of the port's major timber importers, leased storage space on land adjacent to the Hull & Barnsley docks. Pictured in the vicinity of the Horsley area is Hull & Barnsley shunting engine No.1. Built by Beyer Peacock in 1884, Class G1 (originally Class A) 0-6-0T, locomotive No.1 was the first of twelve similar engines ordered by the Hull & Barnsley to a design by William Kirtley. After giving some thirty-seven years service, engine No.1 was retired in 1922.

NEW YORK CORNER

...."Hull is Wilsons and Wilsons is Hull"

'New York Corner, Alexandra Dock, Hull'. Wilson Shipping Line passenger cargo steamer, SS IDAHO, is seen on this official Hull & Barnsley postcard view unloading cargo at the Company's Alexandra Dock, 1908. Built in 1898, and used as one of the Wilson's weekly steamer sailings to New York, the IDAHO was part of their large fleet to use the deep water dock. Described as the finest on the East coast, the dock was able to accommodate deep draft cargo vessels such as the IDAHO. Wilsons joined forces with the Furness Company in 1892 to co-ordinate a regular service from Newcastle, Hull and Southampton. Before the introduction of cargo ships with limited passenger accommodation the vessels on the American run were principally emigrant ships. Before the decline in this trade the main Wilson vessels involved were the CONSUELO, OTHELLO, TORONTO and ONTARIO.

new york corner

Colourful privately owned river craft, together with a solitary North Eastern Railway's lighter, jostle for position alongside an unidentified grain ship berthed at the Hull & Barnsley's Alexandra Docks, 1903. Grain discharging chutes are visible ranged in position on the vessel's starboard side.

Alexandra Dock 'Creek Traffic'. Dating back to ancient times Hull docks enjoyed the unique privilege of being an 'overside port'. The Hull Dock Act of 1774 perpetuated the non levying of charges on goods discharged from ship to river craft. A clause in the Hull & Barnsley Act of 1880 further guaranteed that river carriers using the Company's docks would be exempt from wharfage charges. The term 'Creek Traffic', as it became known, applied to the goods collected by lighters which frequented the Hull & Barnsley and North Eastern Railway's docks. The two companies' lighters were allowed freedom of access into each other's waters. An indication of the volume of 'creek traffic' can be gauged from the number of river craft crowded around the Wilson cargo-emigrant ship SS CONSUELO, pictured at its regular berth at Alexandra Dock, 1903.

DREDGING-MACHINE No.4

Registered in 1914 under the name of H & B Ry Dredger No.4 the new dredging ship was employed in local dock duties. Equipped with a 5-ton Priestman crane grab it could operate in a 26ft radius. With a dredging depth of up to 45ft, 150 tons of silt per hour could be removed. Although the vessel was built in Holland, the dredger's engines were supplied by local manufacturers, Earle's Shipbuilding & Engineering Co., Ltd. After passing into London & North Eastern Railway hands No.4 was occasionally moved up for dredging work at Hartlepools. Reproduced from a Priestman Brothers Ltd., Hull, promotional publication, illustration kindly loaned by Hull Town Docks Museum.

GRAIN SHIPMENT

Tied up in waters adjoining the Alexandra Dock lock-pit, the large passenger-cargo ship, SS GANGES, prepares to discharge its cargo of Indian grain. The vessel berthed alongside the GANGES, emitting a lot of smoke, is the SS CAPULIN making ready to get underway from 'A' jetty. The tug visible passing through the second set of lock-gates from the River Humber is probably on its way to assist the CAPULIN to manoeuvre out of the dock.

LIKE FATHER ...

Alexandra Dock lock-gate men, foreman, berthing men and shunters, c.1908. George Longhorn, grandfather of contributor Peter Longhorn, is pictured standing on the extreme left. The unidentified figure to the right is seated on a Hull & Barnsley timber bogie. At the time of its opening in 1885 the Alexandra Dock lock-pit was one of the largest in the country capable of accommodating the increasing size of steam-ships. The timber and brick accommodation featured in the accompanying photographs are part of a small group of buildings occupied by the Dock Master's offices, situated on the eastern side of the lock entrance.

LIKE SON

Alexandra Dock staff, c.1922. A generation later and George Longhorn's son, Fred, is seen (standing on the right) in the company of, amongst others: Tommy Carter (second from right); unidentified dock agent (wearing trilby hat); dock foreman, Dick Beavers (sporting a walrus moustache). Relations with the Railway appeared to be cordial, almost family affairs, with sons following fathers and even grandfathers in the service of the Company. Photographs courtesy of Peter Longhorn.

BRIDGEWORK....   EASTERN APPROACHES

Bridge No.1' Alexandra Dock, Hedon Road. The Hull & Barnsley's Alexandra Dock was, for a time, one of the largest and best equipped docks in the country. The substantial embankment on which the Railway was built was of immense value in the rapid movement of traffic to and from the dock. Forming a semi-circle around the Hull city centre the emabankment was a prominent local landmark. On leaving Alexandra Dock the Hedon Road bridge was the first of 35 high level bridges encountered within the city boundary. Pictured under the later ownership of the London & North Eastern Railway, the Warren pattern girder bridge is viewed in the direction of the Borough of Hedon in 1934. Behind the hoardings on the right lay the original entrance to the Dock. W. Ward, boot repairer, installed in the tiny building tucked between the advertisements and bridge abutment, carried out his trade in what was the former dock entrance police office.

Hedon Road, January 1988. Demolition men commence to take apart the redundant former Hull & Barnsley Railway Bridge No.1. The decline and eventual closure of 'Alex' Dock inevitably lead to the scrapping of the dock's rail link and attendant bridges. The dismantling of the familiar Hedon Road girder bridge coincided with the removal of other adjoining bridges. Photo courtesy of dockland archivist, Walter Oglesby.

'Five Arches'. A short distance from Alexandra Dock a large bridge complex was situated on the line at Stoneferry. A series of brick arches and plate bridges spanned the North Eastern Railway's line to Hornsea as well as crossing Fordyke Stream at this point. Wending its way across the bridge, outward bound from Saltend, the oil & spirit terminal located to the east of King George Dock, a British Railways petroleum tanker train is seen passing the former Hull & Barnsley's Burleigh Street goods yard signal-box.

Photographed in the 1970s, the northern aspect of the bridge structure shows, to the left, the filled in water course of Fordyke Stream. The river bridge in the foreground which once carried the Hornsea branch line still retains the impression of the former track-bed.

CANNON STREET STATION

CRIMSTON STREET TO **CANNON. St STATION**

A once familiar street sign, situated on the corner of Charlotte Street and Grimston Street, directed intending Hull & Barnsley Railway passengers towards the Company's Cannon Street terminus.

Cannon Street Station, Hull, c1950. Originally designed for use as a carriage shed, the building was adapted to serve as the Company's main passenger station when the scheme for a terminus in the nearby Kingston Square was abandoned in 1884. The many additions and improvements which were carried out to the station in the years 1891 to 1908 included the opening of a W. H. Smith & Company book stall in 1896 and the completion in 1904 of refreshment rooms. In July 1924 the terminus was closed to passengers although it continued to operate as a goods station until final closure in June 1968.

'TREBLE-ONE'

Visible through the industrial haze hanging over the British Gas Light Company's Bankside gas works, the largest of the Company's five gasometers dominates the industrial skyline which overlooks the Hull & Barnsley's Sculcoates Goods Yard. Photographed in c.1908 in the area of the yard adjoining the embankment which carried the Railway's main line through to Alexandra Dock, shunting engine, No.111, appears with an enthusiastic contingent of Sculcoates yard staff. The first of sixteen 0-6-0 tank engines built to Matthew Stirling's new Class G3 design, No.111 was delivered from the Yorkshire Engine Company's Sheffield works in 1901. Handed over to the North Eastern Railway in 1922 and renumbered 3111D, the locomotive was finally absorbed by the London & North Eastern Railway in 1923. Fitted with a domed boiler in 1926, the former Hull & Barnsley 0-6-0T, wearing L&NER No.2492, was eventually withdrawn in September 1937. Photograph courtesy of Tom Makey.

Cannon Street goods sidings, c.1910. Rostered for through freight working, making intermediate stops, Hull & Barnsley Class G3 engine No.143 is pictured with the loco's crew and members of the yard's shunting staff at the Company's depot sidings, Cannon Street, Hull. The need for extra capacity in the period 1895 to 1908 brought about several extensions and additions to the yard's limited siding space. 0-6-0T locomotive, No.143, was the second delivered from an order of ten Class G3 shunting engines manufactured by Kitson & Company in 1908. Wearing trip code number 12, No.143 gently simmers during its photographic encounter. Taken over by the North Eastern Railway at amalgamation in 1922, No.143 continued in service with the London & North Eastern Railway until withdrawal in 1937.

Photo courtesy of the Hull & Barnsley Railway Stock Fund.

Sculcoates Junction Signal-Box. After crossing the River Hull by swing bridge the Hull & Barnsley Railway line entered the extensive Sculcoates goods yard situated just beyond the western bank of the river. Amongst the private works sidings controlled by the Sculcoates junction signal-box were those serving the British Gas Light & Coke Company Ltd. and Hull Corporation Electricity Department. The signal-box illustrated was of an all wood construction, painted brown, and was erected in time for the opening of the line in 1885. The permanent way men and the cabin's signalman appear to be pleased by the occasion, c.1890s.

Photo courtesy of Peter Wilkes collection.

COAL MERCHANTS

Return to Sender'. A typical Hull & Barnsley mineral train consisted of the Company's locomotive, brake van, and assorted coal wagons. Of these, some belonged to the Company as well as a large number of colourful privately owned wagons which were painted in the livery of their particular owners. The importance of the private owner wagon is shown in that by 1923 almost half the total wagons in railway service belonged in private ownership. Although regarded as a sound investment for their owners, private wagons were not favoured by the railway companies as it involved them in the uneconomic practice of, on completion of a delivery, returning empty wagons to their respective owners as quickly as possible.

Unloading household coal from Hull Co-operative Society wagons, Cannon Street station yard, Lockwood Street, Hull, c.1905. Heavily laden with sacks of domestic fuel a Hull Co-op horse and coal rulley, No.22 in the Society's fleet, prepares to set out on its daily coal round from the Hull & Barnsley's Lockwood Street sidings.

Thomas T. Field's, 7 plank, 12 ton mineral wagon, No.8, as it appeared when freshly out-shopped in 1903. Probably the product of local craftsmen, the Field's coal wagon may have been built at one of several Hull wagon builders. Located at Sculcoates Lane for instance were the Kingston Railway Wagon Co. Ltd., and the Midland Railway Carriage & Wagon Co. Ltd. T.T. Field's coal yard was established at Cholmley Street, Hessle Road, Hull.

'Matthews & Son'. Hull coal merchants, H.W. Matthews & Co. Ltd., coal wagons photographed at the North Eastern Railway Company's Botanic Gardens sidings, Prince's Avenue, Hull, 1907. Accompanied by an N.E.R. porter, coal merchant Harry White Matthews is featured with family members on a promotional postcard view of the company's Prince's Avenue depot. Visible at the rear of the Matthews' wagons is a Hickleton Main Colliery mineral wagon. A note on the reverse of the postcard acknowledges a customer's order for Wath best coal. Both Hickleton Main and Wath Main were South Yorkshire collieries connected to the Hull & Barnsley's main railway line.

1914 local directory advertisement for Hull coal merchants, Stonehouse Brothers. Railway coal sidings which the Stonehouse Brothers operated from were located at the North Eastern Railway Company's Temple Street Goods depot and the Hull & Barnsley's Neptune Street Station yard.

BEVERLEY ROAD

Photographed in the early 1960s making its way towards Alexandra Dock, a British Railways Class B1 running tender first eases a tanker train across the railway bridge, Beverley Road. Some twenty years after the bridge's characteristic iron railways were dismantled the structure still retains its original brick and stone parapets. In recent years this top brick and stonework has been replaced by simplified hand railing.
Photo courtesy of Eric Cracknell.

Required by the Hull Corporation to blend with the visual amenities of the area the Hull & Barnsley's magnificent ornamental Beverley Road Bridge is effectively displayed in this 1912 view. Designed by William Shelford, Engineer to the Hull, Barnsley & West Riding Junction Railway & Dock Company, the unique elaborately pierced iron fascia which concealed the railway bridge was visually of exceptionally pleasing design. The coat of arms of the Company, featured in relief, was fixed in the centre of the railings above the main beam.

At the beginning of the Second World War, possibly as a result of the Nation's wartime scrap drive effort, the Beverley Road bridge's cast iron fencing was removed. Photographed in the 1970s, the railway span's bare utilitarian appearance is in marked contrast to the bridge's former Victorian elegance.

Fitzroy Street, Beverley Road. Closed in 1924, the boarded-up remains of the Hull & Barnsley's former Beverley Road Station stand derelict against the skyline. In use throughout the Railway's existence, the station, because of its convenient tram route location, became almost as well patronised as the Company's neighbouring Cannon Street terminus. Demolished in the mid 1980s, the station building was photographed a decade earlier by Martin Barker.

NATIONAL RADIATOR Co.Ltd.

National Radiator Company's Peckett 0-4-0 saddle tank locomotive, No.1056. Pictured in 1906, the year it was placed into service, members of management along with the engine's crew, pose for the obligatory commemorative photograph. Although Hull & Barnsley locomotives were not allowed to run into the Radiator Company's works, the reverse situation existed whereby the Peckett was able to work into the Hull & Barnsley Railway's adjacent Ella Street sidings. During its lifetime the little engine was occasionally to be seen on the Hull & Barnsley main line running light engine towards Springhead for periodic maintenance work.

Fifty years old, and more, and still giving useful service, although a visible sign of wear and tear to the "Peckett" is the loss of its chimney's copper cap. In a bid to improve protection against the vagaries of the English climate the cab of the engine has had additional side sheets fitted. The little shunting locomotive still retains its brass inscribed 'National Radiator Co. Ltd.' nameplate. Mr. J. Banks, Yard Department Manager, and Messrs. Gedney, Taylor and Barwick proudly pose with their charge.

The London based National Radiator Company looked to expand its United Kingdom operation at the turn of the century in view of the increased demand for central heating, largely due to a successful sales campaign. A site at Leeds was at first considered but the Company was eventually persuaded to establish a new works at Hull. Set up in 1906 the plant was designed as a replica of the Company's German factory and occupied a thirty-acre site in what was to become National Avenue. Rail access to the work's sidings was provided by connections from the Hull & Barnsley's Ella Street sidings and the North Eastern Railway Company's sidings at Cottingham South Junction. Thus was formed an unofficial link, through the Radiator Works, between the two rival Railway Companies.

The author is indebted to Harry Jordan, Alan Beacock and Ideal Standard Ltd. for their valuable contribution of photographs and information for the accompanying National Radiator Company article.

The Yard Department's sidings at the National Radiator Company's works dealt with the receiving and marshalling of loaded wagons of pig iron, scrap, coke, sand etc. Once the contents of these wagons had been discharged into their respective bins and allocated places throughout the factory the empty wagons would then be returned to the Department's sidings. In this 1930s view of the yard, loaded wagons of the Southern Railway, London Midland & Scottish Railway and the London & North Eastern Railway are visible behind the large open stock piles of furnace coke.

Assorted Railway Company wagons loaded with finished castings await collection by the Radiator Company's works shunting engine.

SPRING BANK WEST

Spring Bank West Bridge viewed towards Springhead. Constructed in the 1880s it was the next major crossing west of Beverley Road. Creating an overall neat appearance the cast iron columns supporting the bridge girders are complemented by decorative stone and brick parapets. Adding to the general lay-out of the railway bridge are signals and a profusion of telegraph poles. Visible through the bridge in this 1930s view is the former North Eastern Railway Company's signal box which controlled the Hessle Road-Cottingham branch line level crossing. Heading in opposite directions beneath the bridge are Hull Corporation Transport buses, service No.11.

HULL *from the Air.*

On the banks of the River Humber, featured in this 1920s aerial photograph, is the area of land, situated between the Humber Dock to the east and the William Wright Dock to the west, on which some of the important developments of Hull's railway system took place. In July 1840 the City's first railway, the Hull & Selby, opened for passenger and parcels business. The Company's Hull terminus was located on a small site in the appropriately named Railway Street, facing the Humber Dock. The Hull & Selby was eventually taken over by the North Eastern Railway and the site of the terminus was progressively englarged and developed into the large multi-gabled goods depot, (visible to the right of centre in the accompanying illustration). The Lancashire & Yorkshire Railway was represented in Hull with premises adjacent to the North Eastern's depot in Railway Street. In the mid 1860s the Manchester, Sheffield & Lincolnshire Railway is recorded as having a goods depot and warehouse established on the Humberside site, facing Limekiln Creek and Wellington Street, west. In later years the MS&LR was to open a triple gabled goods station in Kingston Street (visible to the left of centre). The MS&LR assumed the title of Great Central Railway in 1899. To the east of their goods station are to be seen the North Eastern Railway's Kingston Street engine shed, built on the site of the old Hull gaol, and warehouses. Further to the west, along the Humber bank, the Hull & Barnsley Railway's Neptune Street depot opened for goods traffic in 1885. The peak of railway expansion in the area illustrated was reached in 1906 when the North Eastern Railway commissioned its new Riverside Quay. Approximately one mile of the Quay's one and a half mile length is visible fronting onto the waters of the Albert Dock.

NEPTUNE STREET

Official interior view of the Hull & Barnsley Railway's chief city goods station, Neptune Street, 1907. In the years 1905/1906 it was apparent that the station's facilities were stretched to the limit. In its twenty years of operation the depot's tonnage of traffic handled had increased to more than double. It catered for all the docks west of the River Hull as well as handling the town's general merchandise traffic. The largest of the Company's three principal Hull goods stations, Neptune Street depot was situated alongside the original Hull & Selby railway line, near to the Kingston Street station. Constructed of brick the building featured triple gables and was thirteen bays in length. Of the five tracks which ran into the premises three were routed through round-arched openings in the centre block whilst single lines entered through two outer wings. Amongst the many items of interest visible in the main warehouse were wagon turntables and a number of electric cranes, installed new in 1906. Traffic continued to increase and it was necessary to expand the depot's facilities, construction being carried out for a number of years until 1915.
Illustration courtesy of the Christopher Ketchell Collection.

ANLABY ROAD

Access to the busy Neptune Street depot was gained by a divergence at Spring Bank North Junction. The high level route which curved away from this point continued via Spring Bank South Junction, across Anlaby Road, Boothferry Road and Hessle Road. A short distance from Hessle Road bridge the line dropped away, down a 1 in 120 gradient, to eventually join the Neptune Street Goods Station. The suburban Anlaby Road crossing point, pictured on a quiet day in the 1930s, is viewed towards the Hull City centre. Spring Bank South Junction was located immediately to the North of the bridge, at the rear of dwellings on the Eastern side of Hamlyn Avenue. Hull Brewery Ales advertisements were a familiar local feature on Hull & Barnsley railway bridge sites.

SPRINGHEAD

Eastern end of Springhead running shed, c.1910. Mineral traffic Class A 0-8-0, No.126, cautiously emerges as a shunting duty Class G2 0-6-0T, running tender first, makes a hurried exit past an out of steam heavy shunting Class F1 0-6-2T. When the Hull & Barnsley Railway opened for traffic in July 1885 it had 42 locomotives based initially at the Hull end of the line. The Company provided itself with an engine shed and maintenance facilities to the west of the city. Capable of housing 36 locomotives the original depot was intended to be built on the triangle of land bounded by the Railway's North, West and South Spring Bank Junctions. As a result of opposition from an adjoining landowner the Company's principal locomotive shed and marshalling sidings were sited on open agricultural land near Springhead Waterworks. The completed establishment took the name of the waterworks and became known as Springhead.

Locomotive Department brass pay check, No.168, embossed with the Railway's full original title, c.1890s. In June 1905 the Company name was officially shortened to the more manageable 'Hull & Barnsley Railway.

'Last of the few'. Fresh out of the paint shop, London & North Eastern Railway J28 Class, No.2409, appears resplendent in front of Springhead coaling stage, c.1930. Originally Hull & Barnsley Class L1 (No.17), it was the second of a delivery of five built in 1911 all fitted with Phoenix superheaters. A further five were received in 1912 from the makers, Kitson & Company, fitted with alternative saturated boilers. Designed by Matthew Stirling the L1 class was a larger more powerful version of his earlier 1888 mineral traffic Class B. In all twenty Class L engines were built between 1911 and 1915. Fitted with a domed boiler in the late 1920s No.2409 served with the L&NER from the grouping in 1923, hauling goods and later mixed traffic until withdrawal in October 1938. Ex-No.17 gained the distinction of being the last surviving Hull & Barnsley tender locomotive, remaining in use at Darlington Works as a stationary boiler until June 1939. It survived for a time out of use before it was eventually broken up later in the year.

185ft in length, situated near the west end of the erecting shops, Springhead's elevated coal stage was first brought into use in July 1908. Proposed and sanctioned the previous year, the new coaling stage was similar in design to the one at the Great Northern Railway's New England Sidings, Peterborough.
Photographed 60 years after it was first commissioned, although in a rundown condition, the building still remains an impressive structure.
Photo courtesy of Brian Latus.

'156'

'Working day'. Class F3 0-6-2T engine, No.156, pictured at Newport Station, bank-top siding, on routine shunting operations, seen here in the process of making up a mixed freight train formation before being forwarded on to Hull docks. The white daubing evident on the leading cattle wagon suggests the use of an antiseptic lime-wash. At amalgamation in 1922, 40 cattle vans on stock with the Hull & Barnsley Railway were transferred into North Eastern ownership.

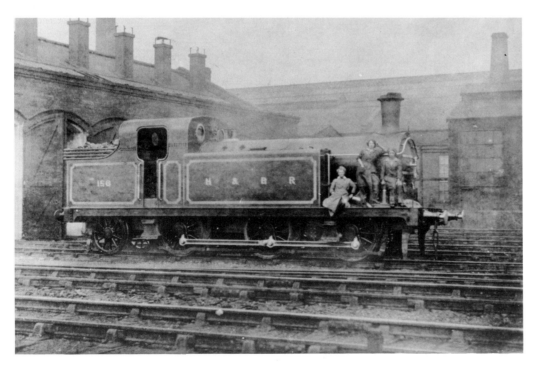

'Rest day'. Photographed at the eastern end of Springhead locomotive sheds, c.1918, No.156 groomed and polished displays the results of the depot's hard working women cleaners. Built by Hawthorn Leslie, No.156 was usually stationed at Springhead. The last of a batch of ten delivered in 1914 this engine was to soldier on until retirement at Leeds in 1955. The small corrugated iron building on the right was the hot water boiler house used for washing out locomotive boilers.
Photo courtesy of Martin Barker.

Express cleaners'. Younger members of Springhead shed staff, grouped along the running-plate of Hull & Barnsley express passenger 4-4-0 Class J, No.33 proudly show off the polished results of their labours. Springhead engine cleaners' rates of pay and conditions are recorded in 1912: commencing at the age of sixteen, ten shillings could be expected for working a fifty three hour week. At the age of twenty-two a maximum of one pound per week was achieved.
Details worthy of attention in this excellent c.1917 view of Springhead yard include an H&BR open goods wagon containing lime overshadowed by the depot's original water tank mounted on heavy timber trestling.
Photo courtesy of C. & L. Collingwood.

SPRING CLEAN

'They also serve'. Suitably attired in mob-caps, coat overalls and trousers, Springhead women cleaners, colleagues of Ethel Collingwood (third from left), line up in 1918 as though to acknowledge their part in helping to keep the wheels of the Hull & Barnsley turning during the years of the Great War. Photo courtesy of C. & L. Collingwood.

'Daily' service. Mob-capped women cleaners attend to their regular carriage cleaning chores, Springhead, c.1916. World War 1 recruitment of women workers was encouraged by the Hull & Barnsley as replacements for many of the railwaymen who were called to the armed forces. Of the Company's three and a half thousand male workforce employed at the outbreak of war over a third joined the Colours.

Receiving the attentions of the cleaning ladies' buckets and brooms is a 1st/3rd semi-corridor brake composite, one of four similar bogie coaches ordered from the Birmingham Railway Carriage & Wagon Company in 1909. With the purchase of a petrol-engined vacuum cleaner for the valeting of coaching stock all carriage cleaning was transferred from Cannon Street in 1912 to a new siding, especially installed for the purpose, at Springhead.

'TINIES'

'Stirling work'. Trees bare of leaves, pale sunlight reflecting off a polished boiler and a wisp of steam hanging in the crisp winter's air suggest the prospect of a chilly turn of duty for the fireman trimming coal on the tender of a Hull & Barnsley Class A 0-8-0, No.124. Pictured after a recent visit to the nearby coaling stage the large mineral traffic locomotive is seen preparing to return to main line duties.

Positioned on Springhead's 55ft turntable the engine's overall size and spotless condition are shown to advantage. Designed by Matthew Stirling, Locomotive Superintendent to the Hull & Barnsley, fifteen Class A members were built in 1907 by the Yorkshire Engine Company. Regular drivers who operated the big 0-8-0s were: Welthorne (117); Corbett (118); Arnott (119); Taylor (120); Haycock (121); Copeland (122); Wilson (123); spare engine (124); Wordsworth (125); Boyle (126); Richards (127); Medd (128); Mitchelson (129); Wride (130); and Tasker (131). As well as serving with the H&B, No.124 continued with the North Eastern Railway (No.3124) and London & North Eastern Railway (No.2505) until withdrawal in 1931.

In not quite the pristine condition of the Class A in the previous illustration, No.118 appears at a later date bereft of decoration save for the locomotive's plain cabside number. It is probable No.118 was photographed at a time when the Hull & Barnsley was about to be absorbed by the North Eastern Railway in 1922. No.118 survived, as did all the members of the class, until 1931. Successive numbers carried by No.118 were 3118D (North Eastern) and 2499 (London & North Eastern).

When first introduced in 1907 the bulky size of the Class A engines prompted their crews to humorously nickname them 'Tinies'. Working the heavy locomotives, however, was quite another matter, and additional pay incentives were necessary to get the men to operate them. A combination of weight and length restricted the big 0-8-0s to working the main line between Springhead and Wath on Dearne. London & North Eastern Railway Class Q10, No.2510, ex-Hull & Barnsley (No.129), is observed in un-rebuilt condition, in the mid 1920s, at the east end of Springhead Works in the company of a rebuilt former H&B Class B, (No.55), L&NER Class J23, No.2436.

Out-shopped London & North Eastern Class Q10, No.2509, ex H&B Class A, (No.128), in rebuilt condition, February 1925. Alterations to the original H&B design include the cab roof extended over the footplate, the original double spectacle cab windows altered to one large window on each side, new domed boiler, North Eastern pattern smokebox door and Ross 'pop' safety valves fitted in place of the original Ramsbottom type. Additional sanding was provided on the second pair of coupled wheels (driving). With the successful introduction of the 04 (ex-ROD) 2-8-0s of Great Central design the days of the former Hull & Barnsley class were numbered. By the end of 1931 the entire fifteen 0-8-0s had been withdrawn from service.

CARRIAGE & WAGON

Group photograph of Springhead Carriage and Wagon Department staff, c.1912. Centrally seated amongst the 90 or so apprentices and time-served men is the dappper bowler-hatted figure of William Jabors Adcock, carriage and wagon works' foreman. The get-together of the department's staff is believed to be on the occasion of the retirement of Mr. Adcock.

When Matthew Stirling departed from the Great Northern Railway in 1885 to take up the post of Locomotive Superintendent with the Hull & Barnsley Railway he brought with him a number of Great Northern railwaymen. At one point in his career on that Railway he held a position at Nottingham and it was from here that William J. Adcock journeyed when he joined Matthew Stirling's workforce at Springhead.

Photograph and information courtesy of Christopher Young, great-great-grandson of William Jabors Adock.

LOCOMOTIVE WORKS

1925 interior view of Springhead's new three road erecting shop with former Hull & Barnsley and North Eastern types undergoing major overhauls. The construction of an annexe to the original erecting shop of 1887 was suggested in 1910, but it was not until 1914 that a tender for £3,920 was accepted. Up to twelve complete locomotive overhauls could be comfortably accommodated in each of Springhead's erecting and fitting shops. At the end of the Hull & Barnsley's independent existence in 1922 the locomotive works had a total of approximately 330 employees and were able to undertake up to 50 heavy repairs and around 30 light repairs annually.

WAGON WORKS

Pictured in the vicinity of the boiler shop, a Class K 0-4-0 shunting locomotive's boiler, out of its frames, acts as makeshift seating for some of the adult staff and boy apprentices assembled for a local photographer on a special occasion in 1902. Seated on the front row, to the right, is William John Adcock, grandson of wagon works foreman, William Jabors Adcock.
Photograph courtesy of Christopher Young.

Composite view of the east end of Springhead Works Yard. Situated at the north east corner of the twenty acre site is the twin-gabled wagon works building of 1897. Six repair tracks accommodated up to 100 vehicles at any one time. Located to the rear of the wagon works was the blacksmith's shop and boiler house. Visible to the right of centre is the three road, single-gabled brick carriage shop completed in 1912.
Photographic sequence courtesy of Brian Latus.

Making a dignified appearance in 1912, a party of carriage and wagon staff assemble in front of one of the pairs of double doors, seen in the open position in the accompanying wagon works illustration. Photograph courtesy of the Hull & Barnsley Railway Stock Fund.

Sharply in focus, this excellent close up of 0-6-0 Class B, No.137, is typical of the many superb photo-studies of Hull & Barnsley locomotives taken by anonymous cameramen at Springhead in the near 90 years of its existence. Photographed in un-lined condition in 1908, the year of its construction by Kitson & Company, No.137 is pictured in the shadow of the yard's timber trestle-mounted water tank. Points of interest in the background include the dismantled cab from an 0-6-0 Class E, the depot's other water tank mounted on a brick base and the newly commissioned coal stage. Renumbered (2518) and reboilered as Class J23 by the L&NER in 1924, ex-No.137 remained in service until November 1937.

'Under new management'. Built in 1914 by the Yorkshire Engine Company for the Hull & Barnsley Railway, former Class L, (No.161), is observed in ex-paint shop condition under the later ownership of the London & North Eastern Railway. Rebuilt with a domed boiler in 1928, L&NER Class J28/2, No.2542, was one of a limited number of its class fitted with vacuum brakes and screw couplings which enabled it to work passenger trains at times of engine shortage. After a relatively short period of 23 years in service ex-H&B No.166 was withdrawn in 1937.

CLASS J... limited edition

The power and the glory of 55 tons of tractive energy are captured in a fine study of Class J, No.38. Viewed alongside Springhead boundary fence, the clean purposeful lines of the Hull & Barnsley's crack express engine are seen to advantage in this c.1912 illustration. Constructed by Kitson & Company in 1910, No.38 was the second of a limited batch of five Class J members built to the design of Matthew Stirling, specifically for the Company's Sheffield passenger service. On the odd occasion Class J locomotives worked outside the H&B system. An example of this was the through working by No.38 of an excursion train to Aintree for the 1920 Grand National. No.38 was unique amongst its class as being, on amalgamation in 1922, the only member to receive the full North Eastern express engine livery of Saxony green. At an earlier date the armorial device of the Hull & Barnsley is seen displayed on the leading splasher of the all black 4-4-0, the only class to receive this heraldic decoration.

Built to a design by William Kirtley, 0-6-0 Class B, No.17, was constructed by Beyer Peacock & Company in 1884. Pictured in rebuilt form as Class E, No.17, fitted with a domeless boiler in 1899, it still retains its original cab. Placed on the duplicate list in 1911 as No.17A, the 0-6-0 was finally withdrawn in 1917. Seen in the background is the works' new boiler shop.
Photo courtesy of the Hull & Barnsley Railway Stock Fund.

'Code of practice'. At first glance Class L1, No.29, would appear to be another new locomotive brought out for the camera to record its delivery in 1912. Closer examination of the pristine 0-6-0, however, reveals white headlamps positioned above the front buffer beam, indicating the engine is in service and rostered for the working of mineral or freight traffic.

ACCIDENT at LOCOMOTIVE JUNCTION

December 1906. Wrapped up against the cold, curious onlookers gather to watch the operation to right the engine and tender of a Hull & Barnsley Class B, 0-6-0, which has fallen down the embankment at Locomotive Junction, Springhhead. Stripped of all removable weight, chains and steel cables take the strain as the slow process of righting the toppled loco on to temporary trackwork begins. When the mishap occurred the locomotive was running tender first under the guidance of driver A. Hill. As a result of the accident he was reduced to fireman in January 1907 and was not reinstated as a driver until April 1913. At the time of the incident as the engine plunged down the embankment at the end of the siding, the driver and fireman, although they managed to scramble clear, were not lucky enough to avoid falling into the lime sludge from the nearby water softening plant, thus emerging covered from head to foot in white residue. Evidence of the force of the impact can be gauged from the amount of brickwork dislodged from the bridge abutment at the intersection of Springhead Lane.

KIRTLEY COLLECTION

Before the opening of the Hull & Barnsley Railway, William Kirtley, Locomotive Superintendent of the London, Chatham & Dover Railway, was engaged as temporary Consulting Engineer pending the engagement of the new company's own Locomotive Superintendent. Original amongst the designs selected by William Kirtley was his passenger Class C, 2-4-0. Built by Beyer Peacock & Company, ten Class C types (Nos.33-42) were delivered in 1885. Rebuilt in 1901-1903 with a Stirling domeless boiler, No.36 was to spend its days working solely with the Hull & Barnsley. At amalgamation with the North Eastern Railway in 1922, with the exception of the previously withdrawn No.38, the entire exhausted class was taken out of service.
Photo courtesy of Eddie Holland.

Although the only passenger type on the Hull & Barnsley until 1910 was the Kirtley Class C 2-4-0s, it is evident from the accompanying illustration that they were available for freight duties as well. Pictured at Springhead in the days before its rebuild in 1901-1903, No.39 is seen wearing trip code No.173 and headlamp code suggesting it to be working a fish, meat or fruit train or an express cattle or express freight train.

Photo courtesy of the Hull & Barnsley Railway Stock Fund.

Transformed almost beyond recognition, a former Kirtley Class C is photographed at Springhead in front of the old machine shop. Endeavouring to raise steam No.38 livens things up by putting on the blower. Rebuilt by Matthew Stirling in 1904 as Class H1, refinements to the 2-4-0 include a 5ft diameter domeless boiler, new rounded cab, smokebox, chimney and buffers. No.38 was placed on the duplicate list (38A) in 1910 and was withdrawn in 1917.

Photo courtesy of the Hull & Barnsley Railway Stock Fund.

LONG DRAG

'Scaling the heights'. Double heading empty coal wagons, Class 04 (ex-ROD) 2-8-0s make an impressive sight as they storm the 1 in 110 gradient which will take them from Springhead up to the summit at Little Weighton. The arrival in 1929 of two of the Great Central designed 2-8-0s for trials on the former Hull & Barnsley system proved so successful that within a year nineteen of the class were allocated to Springhead, and four to Cudworth. The introduction of the Great Central locomotives witnessed the rapid removal of former Hull & Barnsley 0-6-0 and 0-8-0 mineral engines still remaining on the line.

POSTHASTE

Hull, Barnsley & West Riding Junction Railway & Dock Co., parcel stamps. Halfpenny carmine, penny brown and twopenny green examples from the 1885 issue which included a threehalfpenny blue and threepenny blue.

On 1 February 1891, an agreement with the Postmaster General enabled railways to accept letter post for onward transmission. These were obliged to display the normal penny stamp as well as the authorised one issued by the railway company. The design of the railway's stamps was chosen by the Post Office. The Hull & Barnsley Company twopenny green illustrated, post marked Hull 1904, is from the 1897 issue.

'Night Mail'. Responding to complaints from local tradesmen the Hull & Barnsley introduced a Night Mail service in 1896 which was able to guarantee early morning delivery of consigned parcels. For most of its existence the mail train departed from Cannon Street Station at 11.00 each week-night. Operating for over twenty years the service was discontinued in 1917 and was never resumed. Payment by the G.P.O. for the carriage of mails was never very lucrative. The maximum the Hull & Barnsley received in a year was £150. In 1916 between Kirk Smeaton and Carlton, Jack Hudson, for many years driver of the Night Mail, was reputed to have achieved 80 m.p.h., the highest recorded speed on the Railway.

WATER WORKS

The completion of Hull Corporation's Springhead Waterworks in the early 1860s provided the citizens of Hull with an abundant supply of fresh clean water. In 1865, soon after its official opening, it was recorded that six-and-a-half million gallons a day were being pumped to the surface. The Hull & Barnsley undertook to transport coal for the waterworks, and to effect this a single track and siding were connected from the Company's Springhead yard. Access was gained via a break in the depot's perimeter fence. Power to operate the pumping station's large single cylinder vertical steam engine was obtained from four coal-fired Lancashire Boilers, located in the building, visible to the left of the boiler house chimney. To the right of the main building can be seen water workers' cottages. Today steam power has disappeared, and the pumping station extracts water by means of diesel power.

ANLABY

The Hull & Barnsley Railway was laid out as a first-class passenger line. The care and attention which went into its construction is illustrated by the nicely proportioned brick bridge which carried the line across Spring End Lane (later renamed Wolfreton Road), Anlaby.

High summer, 1940. Elsewhere the Battle of Britain is being fought but on this peaceful summer's day the only sound to disturb the neighbourhood of Anlaby is the arrival of L&NER Sentinel steam railcar, 'High Flyer', whose passengers are seen alighting at Springhead halt. Opened by the L&NER in April 1929, the halt was built to serve the village of Anlaby and railwaymen's cottages near the embankment. Steam railcars were introduced into regular passenger service on the former Hull & Barnsley line by the L&NER in the late 1920s and continued in operation until after the end of the Second World War.
Illustration by permission of Mrs. J. Young.

WILLERBY & KIRK ELLA

'The Village Pond, West Ella', official view-card issued by the Hull & Barnsley Railway. Although not directly connected to the Railway, West Ella village, one mile distant from the Company's Willerby & Kirk Ella station, was considered close enough to warrant promotion in advertising literature. The scarcity of travelling public carried by the Railway caused the Company's Officers to look at any worth-while method of encouraging passenger traffic.

Main Street, Willerby, 1915. Dressed for a day in the country Willerby residents off on a day's outing, are pictured making their way towards the Hull & Barnsley's Willerby & Kirk Ella station. Visible through the trees the railway crosses the main road by way of a panelled girder bridge.

Willerby . The station . (1)

Willerby & Kirk Ella station forecourt. Intending passengers approach the Hull & Barnsley Railway's booking office. The substantial main building, pictured in 1910, was built at ground level on the Willerby village side of the railway embankment. Access to the Hull platform (Down line) was by staircase, entered through the booking hall. Travelling time to the City was usually in the order of 10 minutes (Beverley Road Station) and 15 minutes (Cannon Street terminus). Admission to the Up line platform, situated on the Kirk Ella side of the embankment, was by way of a tiled subway. A waiting shed was provided for the convenience of the west bound traveller. The ivy covered portion of the station building was part of the living accommodation occupied by the Stationmaster, William Ashbridge.

Pictured in the early 1900s, the Hull & Barnsley Railway crosses at high level over an unmetalled Beverley Road, Willerby. Items of interest connected with the Railway include a permanent way man crossing the panelled girder-bridge in the direction of Willerby station Home signal. Set at danger, the Up line semaphore signal is visible over the roofs of the row of neat railwaymen's cottages. The local telegraph boy and his dog complete the scene.

Before the opening in 1929 of Springhead Halt, Willerby & Kirk Ella was the first stop on the Hull & Barnsley line west of Hull. A little under five miles away from the bustle of the City, the station's Down platform enjoys a quiet interlude before the arrival of the next Hull bound passenger train.

Broken windows, and empty hallways that no longer echo to the sounds of the everyday activity of a suburban railway station, such was the fate of the Willerby & Kirk Ella station in the mid 1960s.
Photo courtesy of Brian Latus.

LITTLE WEIGHTON CUTTING

Little Weighton Cutting, near Skidby. A Thompson Class B1, in charge of a through freight train, drifts under the chalk cutting's occupation bridge towards Willerby & Kirk Ella station. Pictured at its deepest point, the impressive sheer-sided walls rise to a height of 83ft. This major piece of civil engineering was considered by the Hull & Barnsley management to be an important tourist attraction.

Photographed at the same location within a few years of the closure of the line, the problems the cutting experienced from frost damage are illustrated by the amounts of loose chalk which have fallen onto the track-bed. In winter months, there was also the likelihood of the cutting becoming blocked following heavy falls of snow.

LITTLE WEIGHTON

Track maintenance men, Down line, Little Weighton station, 1908. Situated 9 miles from the Hull terminus, Little Weighton station was constructed in the manner of the majority of the Railway's substantial buildings, in red engineering brick, the designs of which were influenced by the Queen Anne Revival style. It is possible that the rambler roses, visible on the gabled two storey station house, are examples of a variety of pink rose specially named after the first Chairman of the Company, Colonel Gerard Smith. Arthur Marritt was Stationmaster here from the turn of the century up until 1914. In 1909 a fatal accident occurred when single line working was in operation between Little Weighton and South Cave. A gang of five plate-layers working in Drewton tunnel relaying track were run into by an engine returning on the wrong track. One man was killed and another seriously injured.

Little Weighton

Station staff at Little Weighton, 1920. John Dobson was the Stationmaster from 1920 until the early 1930s. Standing, left to right: R. Lewis (porter), E. Oliver (porter), seated left to right: Tom Walker (booking clerk), John Dobson (stationmaster), W. King (lamp man). Photograph believed to have been taken the year John Dobson became Stationmaster. Prior to this appointment he had been Stationmaster for a number of years at the Hull & Barnsley's Beverley Road station, Hull.
Photo courtesy of Martin Barker.

1970s view of Little Weighton station. The former neat Victorian railway halt is now converted to commercial accommodation. Lifted are the railway tracks, and the only traffic using the former track-bed are heavy lorries hauling out limestone from the nearby chalk quarries. Also disappeared are the station signs which advised, 'Passengers must cross the Line by the (road) Bridge'.

AMBULANCE TRAIN

Accident rehearsal. The formation in 1908 of a Division of the St. John Ambulance Brigade at the Neptune Street depot prompted the Hull & Barnsley management to think of trying out the effectiveness of the division in an emergency. In 1912 the Company dispatched an ambulance train to Little Weighton to put to the test the Brigade's first aid facilities. A large formation made up of bogie coaching stock sped to the scene of a supposed rail accident pulled by one of the new Class J, 4-4-0, express locomotives. The leading carriage featured in the formation is a lavatory brake 3rd (semi-corridor) built in 1909 by the Birmingham Railway Carriage & Wagon Company. It is fortunate that of the three examples constructed for the H&B one has survived and is preserved by the Hull & Barnsley Railway Stock Fund organisation at the North Yorkshire Moors Railway station, Goathland. Noted standing in front of the cab of the Class J, No.38, is the Little Weighton Stationmaster, Arthur Marritt.
Photograph courtesy of the Hull & Barnsley Railway Stock Fund.

DREWTON

Set on the edge of the Yorkshire Wolds the picturesque countryside around Drewton Dale was featured in advertising literature published by the Hull & Barnsley to promote the scenic attractions along the route of the Railway.

Drewton tunnel airshaft, Riplingham, one of five brick lined air-vents which followed the route of Drewton tunnel. An incident occurred during the construction of the tunnel when a party of invited guests on a tour of inspection were trapped below ground. The visitors' problems began when their exit was blocked as a result of a thunderstorm developing over the site. At the height of the storm, obliged to vacate the workings, the party were winched up to the surface, riding through one of the airshafts under construction in a contractor's bucket. The chalky nature of the soil is well illustrated by the quantity of chippings which scatter the area.

Drewton tunnel entrance, east end. 1 mile 354 yards in length, the tunnel was the longest on the Hull & Barnsley Railway. Only the entrance sections and roof curvatures were brick-lined, the side walls remained bare due to the hardness of the chalk rock. Situated a short distance beyond Little Weighton station, Drewton Tunnel marked the summit of the line.

SOUTH CAVE

'Away-day'. Dressed in their Sunday best and eagerly anticipating the day ahead, Hull Sunday School pupils and teachers, on a sixpenny day excursion, pose for an outing photograph at the Hull & Barnsley's South Cave Station, c.1905. With the trippers' picnic hampers safely loaded on to a local carrier's horse and rulley, a station porter, seated with the cart driver, prepares to accompany the excursion to a local beauty spot, the celebrated St. Austin's Rock at Drewton. Visible near to the station's water crane, Stationmaster H. Spencer watches the proceedings with a keen interest. Mr. Spencer was Stationmaster at South Cave from the turn of the century until the mid 1920s. His station residence was an impressive affair, half timbered, twin gabled with pierced barge boards. South Cave was the largest village on the Railway's route. Local passengers however were faced with a mile walk to the station. Facing a longer journey were the great-grandparents of the first United States president, George Washington, believed to have lived in South Cave before they departed for America in 1657.

South Cave

Comings and goings, South Cave station c.1910. An 0-8-0 Class A hauling a heavy train of best Yorkshire coal takes a breather before tackling the long 1 in 150 climb from South Cave up to the summit at Little Weighton. Pausing on the Up line to take water, an 0-6-0 heads a seemingly endless train of returning empty private owner wagons.

Former South Cave station viewed from the Market Weighton road bridge in the 1970s. The single storey building, seen in close-up on the previous page, formerly housed a porters' room, lavatories and storeroom. At this particular time the station buildings and goods yard were being used by a haulage concern. Recently the station building has been cut back in size following the demolition of the flat roofed section.

NORTH CAVE

Ex-North Eastern Railway's 0-4-4T, Class G5, lingers at North Cave Station with a Howden-Hull two coach push-and-pull set. From 1932 all passenger trains on the former Hull & Barnsley route terminated at South Howden.

'Booking Hall'. Photographed in the 1970s the former North Cave station building, built to a similar design to that at Willerby & Kirk Ella, is seen converted to a fine country residence. Occupied at the time by the local doctor, Booking Hall, as it was named, served as accommodation and surgery.

NEWPORT

Three miles on the Up line from North Cave the Hull & Barnsley Railway, immediately after crossing the Market Weighton canal, entered at high level, Newport Station. Perched at the top of the embankment the station's timbered (Down) platform, seen in this c.1908 view, was connected to the main building, which was set at ground level, by means of a long corrugated roofed stairway. A warning bell, positioned on the staircase landing, signalled the approach of passenger trains. The first floor of the station building, visible to the rear of the platform staff, provided living accommodation for the resident Stationmaster and his family. Wearing the Company's distinctive double-breasted frock coat, George Grayson, Newport Stationmaster from 1900 until the 1930s, appears with his children and members of staff, porter Thomas Makey nearest the camera. Newport tended to be one of the Hull & Barnsley's better patronised stations, market-days and Saturdays contributing higher than average revenues. Hay and straw traffic as well as vegetable consignments also contributed valuable earnings. Under the later ownership of the London & North Eastern Railway, the station was renamed Wallington.

Photograph courtesy of Mrs. E. Glen via Tom Makey.

1918. The newest recruit to the ranks of the Newport Station staff, fourteen year old lad porter, Stanley Judson, poses for a souvenir photograph at Seaman's Studios, Hull. The proud possessor of the Company's green corduroy working outfit, young master Judson cuts a dash in front of the camera wearing his brand new Hull & Barnsley Railway uniform.

Photograph courtesy of Tom Makey.

WALLINGFEN GARDENS

Possibly to avoid confusion with the several stations in the United Kingdom identified with the same name, the London & North Eastern Railway, after acquiring the former Hull & Barnsley Railway system in 1923, approved the change of title of Newport Station to Wallingfen. The name adopted by the L&NER was chosen because the station came within the boundaries of the civil parish of Wallingfen.

In the immediate post-war years attractive flower gardens were created from an overgrown plot of land located at the rear of Wallingfen Station. Overrun with wild rose briars, the area was taken in hand by porter Arthur Stephenson and, tended with care and devotion, turned into a veritable Garden of Eden. Such was the quality and originality of his labours that Wallingfen was to win on a number of occasions the 'Best Kept Station Gardens' award. The ultimate accolade was accorded to Arthur Stephenson when coach tour operators began to bring visitors to view the colourful floral displays.

Station porter Arthur Stephenson, creator of Wallingfen's gardens.

Photographs and information generously supplied by Arthur Stephenson.

SANDHOLME

Sandholme Station gardens. Photographed to the west of the main station building, Stationmaster Lawton in the company of the halt's platform staff (porter Harry Wiles, centre) are pictured in a relaxed pose for the camera. The flight of steps leading down from the Gilberdyke road bridge allowed intending passengers access to the Down platform.
Photograph courtesy of Arthur Stephenson.

Marooned in a fenced triangle of land, the remains of Sandholme Station lie within sight and sound of traffic hurrying by on the M62 motorway. A typical Hull & Barnsley country station, its former value to the Railway lay in its extensive marshalling sidings. Lengthy coal trains from the south Yorkshire pits terminated here. The long incoming mineral trains were divided into manageable loads before being dispatched over the summit to Springhead.

HOWDEN

Hull & Barnsley Railway Station, Howden.

Holroyd & Asquith's
Real Photo Series
Copyright.

Howden Station, 1913. Thundering out of the early morning mists which shroud the local countryside, a hard working 0-6-0, Stirling Class B, No.49, heads a Down mineral train in the direction of Sandholme sidings. Built in 1889, No.49 survived in reboilered form until withdrawal in 1926.

"Greenwich Time Is Kept At All Stations"

. . . . . Time Table announcement, Hull, Barnsley, & West Riding Junction Railway & Dock Co., 1885.

Howden

A quarter of a mile or so away from the main station building, the fine Perpendicular style tower belonging to Howden's medieval church rises through the morning mist to dominate the centre of the market town. Grander in design than the majority of the Hull & Barnsley's low level stations, Howden was ranked as a Class 'A' property.

Regarded by the Company as the most important intermediate halt on the Railway's route, Howden Station enjoyed the advantage of a prime location near the centre of the township. Not quite so convenient for the North Eastern Railway's customers was their outlying station situated almost a mile away to the North.

Pictured in 1905, Hull & Barnsley Railway staff outnumber the solitary passenger waiting beneath the larger of Howden Station's distinctive platform awnings. Stationmasters associated with Howden in the pre-grouping years included George Brindle, Alfred Knaggs and James Pearson.

BRIDGE over the RIVER OUSE

OUSE BRIDGE H&B RAILWAY

Four miles to the west of Howden, the Hull & Barnsley Railway line crossed the River Ouse by way of a fine lattice swing bridge. 403ft in overall length and weighing 2,000 tons in the centre span, the river bridge required the services of a signalman, engineman and boilerman. Housing accommodation for the bridge staff was provided on the west bank of the river. Photographed in 1907, facing up stream, a Kirtley 0-6-0 Class B locomotive hauling a mixed train of goods and mineral wagons, outward bound from Cudworth North Junction, clatters at reduced speed across the bridge's steel decking towards the east bank of the river.

CARLTON

'Pouring on the coals'. Drifting smoke obscures the view at Carlton Station as the fireman banks the fire of the recently arrived Stirling 0-8-0. Pictured in the early hours, drawn alongside the Down platform, the splendidly turned out locomotive, No.125, takes on water before continuing its eastward journey at the head of a weighty coal train. The 0-8-0 'Tinies' were capable of hauling from Cudworth, trains of up to 45 fully loaded 10 ton mineral wagons.

Situated approximately 3 miles to the west of the River Ouse, Carlton Station served the nearby villages of Camblesforth and Carlton. A prominent landmark in the vicinity was Carlton Towers, seat of the Beaumont family.

Mindful of the need to promote the tourist potential of the Hull & Barnsley Railway, the Company produced a series of postcard views of scenic areas likely to attract visitors to the line. Of the many picturesque West Yorkshire places the Railway travelled through, the stone craggs overlooking the River Went, and the village road at Went Bridge, featured in the accompanying official illustrations, were depicted as within easy reach of the Railway's Kirk Smeaton Station.

The Craggs, River Went, & Smeaton Church. Kirksmeaton Stn. H & B Ry.

Went Bridge, Kirksmeaton Stn. H & B Ry.

SCENIC DELIGHTS

75

SNOW BOUND

Pictured in the mid 1920s at Springhead, a Hull & Barnsley Class B 0-6-0 tender engine with snow-plough attached is seen on standby duty. In parts the Hull & Barnsley line was particularly vulnerable to heavy falls of snow. Blockages could be for several days at a time, Little Weighton cutting in particular being at risk. To help relieve the situation a snow-plough was stationed at Springhead shortly after the opening of the Railway. Manufactured by Earle's Shipbuilding & Engineering Co. Ltd. of Hull, at a cost of £35, the plough blade was available in early 1886 for mounting on the front of an 0-6-0 engine.

Ten miles on from Carlton, Kirk Smeaton Station was originally laid out as a basic country station with a goods yard at the Hull end of the Down side. Following the opening in 1902 of the Hull & Barnsley's Wath branch line, Kirk Smeaton was upgraded to a terminus for the new branch passenger service. The Up (Cudworth) platform was reconstructed into a bay platform, the outer face of which handled the Wath passenger traffic. A commodious brick and panelled waiting shed provided shelter for both Wath and Cudworth passengers. Viewed across from the island platform the main station building shows the influence of the Queen Anne Revival style in the manner of its construction. Signalling controlled from the unusually positioned platform signal-box includes a paid of ground shunt signals, seen in the foreground set at danger, and, in the distance, a pair of Down (home) signals which controlled entry to the station for incoming through and terminus traffic. Visible between the junction signal and the platform end is the parapet of the short viaduct which carried the line across the River Went and a nearby road. The neat verticle platform railings were replaced at a later date by diagonal fencing. Although the station was built to serve the villages of Little Smeaton and Kirk Smeaton, passenger receipts were never more than modest. In this superbly detailed 1905 view, the bearded figure of Stationmaster E. A. Cousins obligingly poses for the camera whilst the activities of the photographer, Mr. Wales, attract the attention of Kirk Smeaton Box signalman.

'Oiling Round', Kirk Smeaton, 1905. Driver, H. Chester, prepares his Class F2 locomotive, No.109, in readiness for another hard day's labour. Designed for working the short steeply graded colliery branch lines on the western reaches of the Hull & Barnsley Railway, Class F2 0-6-2T engines were capable of hauling a fully loaded coal train up to the main-line junction where a tender locomotive would be attached. The train would then be forwarded on to Hull. Built by Kitson & Co. in December 1901, No.109 was in a serious accident two years after the accompanying photograph was taken. In the early hours of 25 September 1907, at Wath, awaiting the return of the fireman who was collecting the single-line tablet from the nearby signal-box to enable the engine to proceed to Hickleton Colliery, the boiler of No.109 exploded. Although externally there was little sign of damage to the boiler barrel, the force of the explosion lifted the engine off the track. The cause of the disaster was attributed to the failure of a number of firebox stays. No.109's driver, Brooks, died from his injuries. His body was discovered in the Great Central's marshalling sidings 400 yards away. The damaged engine was subsequently repaired and returned to traffic. It was finally withdrawn in December 1936.

Photo courtesy of Derek Vine.

HOLIDAY HAUNTS

The Hull & Barnsley thought it appropriate to promote the opening of the Railway's Wath branch line by publishing this scene of quiet seclusion, set in the West Riding market town of Wath-upon-Dearne. Pictured in the grounds of the former Wath Hall estate, the Town Hall overlooks the Jubilee commemorative fountain of 1887 and the ancient church of All Saints, built in the manner of the late Norman and Early English styles. Opened in 1902, the new 8½ mile freight and passenger line connected the town of Wath into the Hull & Barnsley railway system at Wrangbrook Junction.

In a sylvan setting, the entrance to Brock o' Dale, Kirk Smeaton, is illustrated in this 1907 postcard view, issued by the Hull & Barnsley Railway. Every Thursday, Saturday and Sunday special third class return fares were available for Hull passengers wishing to take advantage of the Railway's "Cheap Excursions to the Country" offer. Destinations featured amongst the Hull & Barnsley day trips included, at a cost of 1/9d, Kirk Smeaton Station (for Brock o' Dale). Prominent in the Company's advertising, the picturesque beauty spot was situated in the Brockerdale valley to the west of Kirk Smeaton, in countryside associated with the legendary Robin Hood.

Monarch of the Glen? Engraver's romanticised view of a J Class 4-4-0 locomotive hurrying its bogie coaching stock through a setting reminiscent of Highland Railway scenery. Illustration reproduced from a c.1910 time table, courtesy Hull Transport Museum.

'Trip Work', Cudworth Yard, 1921. Hull & Barnsley yard staff, buttons and badges polished, take time off from their duties to appear for the camera in front of Cudworth pilot, Class F1 engine No.98. Shunter Sanderson with foot on rail looks on. Employed in the making up of trainloads for Hull, Cudworth Yard's principal commodity was coal. Traffic from the collieries was trip worked by Cudworth pilot engines into Cudworth Yard. The F1 class were the largest tank engines owned by the Railway and well suited for the heavy duty shunting and 'trip' working at Hull and Cudworth. No.98 appears to be finished in a later period unlined livery. Built by Kitson & Co., Leeds, it was kept in service until December 1944. Hull engines of this type were known as 'trawlers', the noise of their whistles being similar to the sound made by the ships' hooters on the local fishing fleet.
Photograph courtesy of Ian Scotney.

CUDWORTH ..... JOURNEY'S END

MIDLAND RAILWAY STATION, CUDWORTH.

"The RAILWAY is in connection with the Midland Railway, at Cudworth, for Passengers, Goods, and Mineral Traffic".... Time Table announcement, 1885.

Connecting passengers arriving at the Hull & Barnsley Railway's Cudworth terminus, after first alighting at the Company's single platform station (pictured extreme right), were obliged to cross over to the Midland Railway platforms via an iron girder footbridge. The Hull & Barnsley single-storey station building was a modest affair. Two outer wings constructed in brick flanked a wooden fronted centre section. Although it was intended at a later date to provide a refreshment room, nothing came of the scheme. Midland Railway staff worked the terminus, and a share of the expenses proportionate to its use were met by the Hull & Barnsley Railway. Cudworth offered connections to Sheffield, the East Midlands, Birmingham, Bristol and the South West. In October 1905 a through service, Hull to Sheffield via Cudworth, was inaugurated. The Hull platform was not used by the service, trains calling at Cudworth utilising the Midland Railway platforms.

CONTINENTAL ROUTE

Acting on a proposal made by the Hull & Barnsley's Goods Manager, Mr. J.W. Shaw, the Officers of the Company agreed to the marking of certain wagons and vans with the legend "CONTINENTAL ROUTE VIA HULL". Following the experimental lettering of a high-sided wagon and goods van in late 1905, the decision was taken to treat other similar items of rolling stock in the same manner, as and when it was practicable to do so. In the accompanying works photograph of a 10-ton fish van, manufactured by the Gloucester Railway Carriage & Wagon Company Ltd. in October 1907, the Continental Route legend, applied by hand in 6 inch white block lettering, contrasts sharply against the van's woodwork colouring of light (teak) brown.

Photograph courtesy of the Hull & Barnsley Railway Stock Fund.

One of the few surviving photographs of a Hull & Barnsley mineral wagon displaying the "CONTINENTAL ROUTE VIA HULL" legend, c.1906. Pictured in the working environment of a Yorkshire colliery, a train of open wagons transporting mining materials is seen in the process of being unloaded in the vicinity of the pit-head buildings. Painted dark grey, the 10-ton Hull & Barnsley wagon loaded with pit props clearly shows the Continental Route legend. Other Railway Company wagons visible in the formation include those of the Great Central. An indication of the increasing prosperity of the Hull & Barnsley Railway can be gauged from the number of assorted open wagons operated by the Company. Of the original 300 delivered in 1885, the number transferred to the North Eastern Railway at amalgamation in 1922 had risen to 3,339.

GENTLEMEN

'Knights of St. John', 1908. Paraded in front of a R.Y. Pickering & Co. manufactured fish van, members of the Neptune Street goods station Division St. John Ambulance Brigade, resplendent in the new Corps uniforms, proudly pose with members of management on the occasion of the inauguration of the depot's Brigade. First aid activities by the Hull & Barnsley work-force were encouraged by the Company's administrators.

AND PLAYERS

'Eleven Plus'. With the blessing of management the Hull & Barnsley Athletic Club was established in December 1910. Eleven acres of land provided by the Company, close to the Ella Street Depot, were approved for use as a sports ground. The provision of a cricket pitch was the club's first priority and was completed in 1911. Players from the Hull & Barnsley 2nd XI cricket team are pictured in 1913 at the ground's sports pavilion. The young man seated cross-legged is proudly displaying a copy of 'The County Pocket Cricket Score Book'. Friendly rivalry existed between the teams of the Hull & Barnsley and the neighbouring North Eastern Railway. Matches between the two were recorded as early as 1885. It is noted that in the 1890s fixtures, the 1st XI team averaged two matches per season against the North Eastern Railway Clerks' Cricket Club.

POLICE BOX

Dock labourers enjoy a midday pipe of tobacco outside the stone sett roadway entrance to the Hull & Barnsley's Alexandra Dock, Hedon Road. Notice boards positioned throughout the dock complex warned, "Smoking Strictly Prohibited by Order of the Dock Superintendent, C.W.B. Anderson". 'Alex' dock workers caught having a quiet smoke would have been requested to report to the dock's police office, located near the Hedon Road entrance. Superintendent Anderson was to lose his life in tragic circumstances in February 1907. Whilst on Company business to the Continent the ferry in which he was a passenger struck the North Pier at the Hook of Holland in the teeth of a gale. The steamship broke in two and foundered with a large loss of life.

Viewed on a pleasant summer day in 1905, a 'Town way Up' wagonette, its horse power drooping between the shafts, lingers in the hope of picking up passengers outside the curiously shaped, hexagonal police office. In later years the dock entrance was resited a short distance away to the west of the original. As a result of the move the police box became redundant and was eventually let off to private traders.

BOYS IN BLUE

A further view of the Alexandra Dock police office finds P.C.21, Harry Wintie, and P.C.24, Harry Smith, officers of the Hull & Barnsley Railway police force, on docks patrol duty, weather-proof capes at the ready. The Railway's constabulary was an early user of police-dogs. P.C.Wintie is believed to have been related to H. Wintie, engine driver, resident in the Beverley Road district, Hull, c.1914.
Photo courtesy of the Hull & Barnsley Railway Stock Fund.

The smartly turned out figure of Hull & Barnsley Railway Police officer, P.C.5, Charles Ladigus presents himself outside the entrance to the Alexandra Dock police office, c.1914. Situated at the rear of the building was a small 'lock-up' constructed to hold suspected miscreants. From 1914 police constable Ladigus was resident for a number of years in Craven Street, Hull.
Photo courtesy of the Hull & Barnsley Railway Stock Fund.

'A RAILWAY SILVER WEDDING'

A Railway Silver Wedding.

Souvenir

OF THE

HULL & BARNSLEY RAILWAY COMPANY'S

"Old Boys" Re-union Dinner

HELD IN THE

Assembly Rooms, Hull,

ON WEDNESDAY, OCTOBER 19th, 1910,

W. S. WRIGHT, ESQ.,

Chairman of the Company Presiding.

Speeches by :—

Lieut.-Col. Sir GERARD SMITH, K.C.M.G.,

W. S. WRIGHT, Esq.,

and others.

Programme cover reproduced courtesy of Hull City Records Office.

October 19th 1910, Jarratt Street Assembly Rooms. 270 men of all ranks gathered at an 'Old Boys' re-union dinner to celebrate 25 years service with the Hull & Barnsley Railway. To qualify, the men had to have joined the Railway before 1886. Of those present, at least eighty had been with the Company at the opening of the line. A further fourteen men had transferred to the line from the contractors constructing the railway. Amongst the old hands assembled was an ex-driver, with whitened hair, whose working days ceased the day his locomotive ran into the rear of a coal train and toppled down an embankment. Dignitaries invited included the Company's directors and officers; Lt. Colonel Sir Gerard Smith, the first chairman of the Company; Vincent Hill, the first manager; and A.C. Hurtzig, the first engineer. Presiding over the evening's events was the chairman of the Company, W.S. Wright. Mingling with the guests of honour was organising committee member John Dodsworth, a distant relative of the author. The substantial dinner was enhanced by music and song provided by the Apollo Glee Singers, with J.W. Fryer as the accompanist. H.F. Fawcett augmented with music on the organ. A commemorative souvenir of the occasion was published, entitled 'A Railway Silver Wedding'. Comparisons were made in the publication between the present day and the situation twenty five years ago regarding traffic, rolling stock, personnel and wages. The piece ended on the note that 'The night was all too short'.

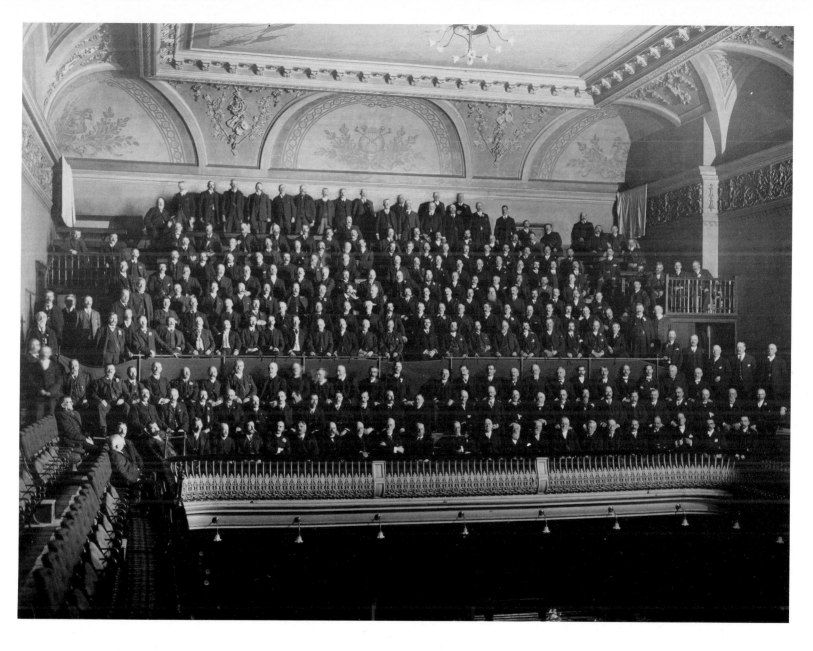

All ranks of past and present staff are pictured, after the re-union dinner, gathered together in the Assembly Rooms' western gallery for a commemorative group photograph. Mr. Drinkwater, of Turner & Drinkwater photographers, officiated behind the camera lens. Photograph courtesy of L.S.R. Baker.

JOINT VENTURE

NORTH EASTERN RAILWAY

AND

HULL & BARNSLEY RAILWAY

Opening
of the
Hull Joint
Dock :: ::

.. BY ..

HIS MAJESTY THE KING

ACCOMPANIED BY

HER MAJESTY THE QUEEN

ON

FRIDAY, 26TH JUNE, 1914

Possibly reflecting the mood of the time, the restrained design of the 1914 Joint Dock celebrations programme was in marked contrast to the florid decoration displayed on the cover of the 1881 ceremonies edition. Reproduction courtesy of Walter Oglesby.

NORTH EASTERN AND HULL AND BARNSLEY RAILWAY COMPANIES.

OPENING of NEW DOCK at HULL
BY
HIS MAJESTY THE KING,
On Friday, June 26th, 1914.

ADMIT BEARER
to
No. 1 Quay.

Alex Wilson.
Secretary Hull Joint Dock Committee.

It is requested that ticket holders be in their places not later than 10-30 a.m.

No. 196

Hull Joint Dock opening ceremony. Before 10.30 a.m. on the great day bandsmen and choristers, holders of white admission tickets, were permitted to proceed to their allotted places on No.1 Quay.
Illustration courtesy of Walter Oglesby.

Powers granted to the Railway Companies of the North Eastern and Hull & Barnsley enabled them to undertake the construction of a jointly owned deep-water dock on land sited to the east of the Hull & Barnsley's Alexandra Dock. Work on the new dock commenced in 1906 and was to eventually cover some 226 acres. The joint venture was completed in 1914. His Majesty King George V, accompanied by Queen Mary, performed the opening ceremony on 26 June 1914.

ROYAL PROGRESS

1.50 p.m. The top-hatted figure of King George, in the company of Queen Mary, prepares to leave the Royal Pavilion at the conclusion of the ceremony to mark the opening of the new King George Dock. It was during His Majesty's speech declaring the opening that he conferred his name on the Dock. As the King and Queen take their leave, an equerry, top-hat in hand, holds open the door of the Monarch's Daimler in readiness to usher their Majesties away to the waiting Royal Train. At 2.00 p.m. the special train departed from the temporary platform, specially erected for the occasion to the north of No.1 Quay.

Obverse and reverse sides of the medallion struck to commemorate the visit to Hull of King George V and Queen Mary on the occasion of the opening of the Hull Joint Dock.

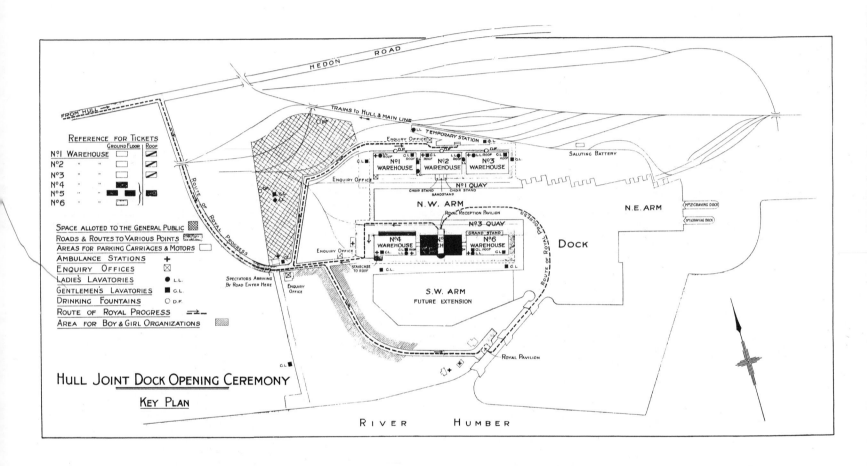

Key plan, Hull Joint Dock opening ceremony, Friday 26 June 1914. Apart from the general public attending in their thousands, special trains brought some 14,000 guests of the Railway Companies to view the proceedings. The dock was brought into operational use on Saturday 1 August 1914. Three days later, on Tuesday 4 August, Britain declared war on Germany and the new dock was requisitioned by the Royal Navy.

FAMILY ENTERTAINMENT

Messrs S. Pearson and Son Ltd., contractors to the King George Dock, entertained the navvies and workmen employed in building the dock, with their wives and children, to dinner at the Jarratt Street Assembly Rooms on the afternoon and evening of the day of the Royal visit. 600 navvies and other workmen, along with their wives and children, brought the total attending the dinner and dance to 1,700. Mr. F.T. Hopkinson, a director of Pearsons, presided over the festivities. Special dispensation was granted by the Pope to members of the Catholic Church attending the celebrations, allowing meat to be consumed on the Friday, the day of the Royal visit.

King George Dock, quay side track renewal. Waiting for materials to be brought up, plate-layers Jack Golding (former Hull Kingston Rovers player) on the left, Harry Norman (sub ganger) in the centre, and Phil Hickson on the right, enjoy a few minutes breather. The title plate-layer originates from the pioneering days of railways when men were sent out to lay the primitive tram-line "plate-ways".
Photo courtesy of Phil Hickson.

PLATE-LAYERS

Alexandra Dock, plate-layers re-laying pointwork. Putting their backs into it, the track maintenance gang include, left to right: John (Phil) Hickson; Jack Longthorne; Sid Newman; Sol King and Harry Norman. The scissors implement operated by Phil Hickson is a sleeper grab, used in the manhandling of heavy wooden sleepers. Baltic fir tended to be the material used in the production of railway sleepers. During their manufacture, to avoid the possibility of rotting, each baulk of timber is immersed in creosote and absorbs up to six gallons in the process.
Photo courtesy of Phil Hickson.

CUTTING CREW

A typical scene illustrating the work involved in excavating a railway cutting. The steam navvy seen in the process of scooping out earth is an early type of rail-borne mechanical excavator. As only the jib boom was pivoted, these early machines were hampered by their limited turning radius which resulted in the need to laboriously draw back and re-set the grab each time a fresh face was to be cut. Later types of excavators had the whole of the working superstructure mounted upon a rotating platform. This method speeded up the work rate considerably as it allowed the navvy to operate to the rear as well as to the front. The crew of three usually required to operate the excavator consisted of a driver, fireman and a young lad to see to the oiling and to keep up the boiler's water-level. The water for the boiler of the machine illustrated is carried in a container mounted on an open wagon. The gang of men visible in the centre of the earthworks are plate-layers waiting their turn to lay rails in front of the excavator when it reaches its maximum digging arc. The rails carrying the steam navvy are positioned down the middle of the cutting, with an additional track at the side to enable the open tipping wagons to remove the excavations. The horse in the picture was used to position individual spoil wagons alongside the working excavator. When fully loaded the wagon would be drawn away by the horse to be marshalled into a train, ready to be hauled away from the cutting site by one of the contractor's locomotives. Spoil wagons used in the construction of the railway were of the side-tipping and end-tipping variety.

MAKING THE GRADE

c.1913. Pictured at an advanced stage of construction the North West Arm, Main Dock and North Eastern Arm of the Joint Dock are all but completed. Midway down the steep incline which gave access to the floor of the new dock, the driver, fireman and boy assistant of the steam navvy, seen at the foot of the incline, spare a moment for the photographer recording events in and around the dock workings. Loaded tipping wagons ascending and empty wagons descending the steep slope to the floor of the dock were rope-worked by stationary steam engine. Visible to the right on No.3 Quay, in the later stages of construction, are warehouses Nos. 4, 5 and 6. No.1 Quay on the left shows warehouses Nos.1, 2 and 3 at a much earlier state of construction.
Photo courtesy of Walter Oglesby.

'Uphill Work'. Viewed from the base of the access gradient, a train of rope-worked tipping wagons on their way out of the dock to deposit their loads are held in check by the contractor's steam powered winding-engine, seen in position at the top of the rise. The chimney and water tank of the steam engine are clearly visible against the skyline as are the contractor's various temporary warning signs, telegraph pole, signal-box etc. Within a few months the unfinished concrete and brick retaining wall, breached to allow freedom of passage to the floor of the dock, would be sealed and the gradient and track-work removed.
Photo courtesy of Walter Oglesby.

King George Dock

WORK HORSE

Contractors S. Pearson & Son Ltd. employed a number of saddle tank locomotives on the Joint Dock project. Purchased from one of the several manufacturers which specialised in this type of industrial locomotive, the inside cylinder 0-6-0 saddle tank engine, CALOW, appears before the camera in surprisingly good condition considering the rough nature of the contractor's working environment. The locomotives were the pride and joy of their drivers and were understandably kept in spotless condition, polished brass and shining paintwork adding the finishing touch to these impeccably maintained machines.
Photo courtesy of Walter Oglesby.

RUNAWAYS

'Rambling Rose'. Joint Dock labourers, working on No.3 Quay, are quickly on the scene to begin the back-breaking task of re-railing the contractor's tank engine, 'ROSE', and its train of mineral wagons which appear to have run into a collapsed embankment. Photo courtesy of Walter Oglesby.

'Rough Treatment'. Runaway contractor's wagons lie in a jumbled heap on the floor of the new Joint Dock. The empty tipping wagons were apparently on their way down the access gradient when the rope hawser restraining the descent of the wagon train gave way. Solidly constructed from stout timbering, the damaged side-tipping wagons, once retrieved, would soon be repaired in the joiner's shop and quickly returned to service. Able to hold three to four cubic yards of spoil, the large carrying capacity and construction of the tip wagons are clearly visible in this detailed view of the mishap.

WOOLLEN TRADE

Wool sheds, King George Dock, 1922. Australian shippers were persuaded by the Hull & Barnsley to route wool shipments through the Hull docks instead of the Pool of London. By 1912, considerable amounts of raw wool began to arrive from New Zealand and Australia. The trade declined during the war years but picked up again after the cessation of hostilities. The increasing imports of wool after the war witnessed the establishment of monthly wool sales. Facilities to handle this trade were provided by the Hull & Barnsley, purchasing and erecting war surplus sheds adjacent to National Avenue, and similarly, the North Eastern Railway purchasing redundant submarine workshops, previously in use on the banks of the River Severn, and siting them near the entrance to King George Dock. Whilst under the later ownership of the London & North Eastern Railway, the corrugated iron wool sheds were badly damaged during the large scale bombing of Hull docks in 1941.

Nissen Huts, King George Dock. Exterior view of Nos. 1 to 18, annexe wool sheds and interior example illustrating warehouse-men accepting bales of wool for storage.

'Pulling the Wool'.
The large volume of raw wool imported from Australia, New Zealand and other sources is graphically illustrated by this interior view of the King George Dock wool sheds showing the huge quantities of wool bales stacked floor to ceiling. With the assistance of a portable winch the wool shed workers demonstrate a deft touch when it comes to handling some of the 140,000 bales of wool stored at any one time in the North Eastern's extensive warehouse.

Approached through an area bordering the neighbourhood of Marfleet, the North Eastern Railway's access to the new Joint Dock was achieved by crossing at high level the main Hull to Hedon Road. Pictured in the 1920s, a Hull Corporation Tramways tramcar makes its way towards the city centre, the power lines for the tram service stretching beneath the centre of the railway bridge. In contrast to the design of the Hull & Barnsley's Alexandra Dock girder bridge, situated further along the road, the North Eastern's contribution is a simple, straightforward affair.

FOREIGN PARTS

Pictured near York in 1923, a Stirling reboilered former Hull & Barnsley 0-6-0, Class B, heads a through freight train, making intermediate stops. The outward appearance of the ex-Hull & Barnsley goods engine is unusual in that although it recently came under the ownership of the London & North Eastern Railway, having passed through the hands of the North Eastern Railway the year previously, the former mineral engine is seen to be still wearing its original Hull & Barnsley loco number, 94. Built by the Yorkshire Engine Company in 1900, No.94 was one of fourteen Class B members sent on loan to the South of England to help alleviate the shortage of light goods engines experienced by the South Eastern & Chatham Railway in the years 1915 to 1919.
Photo courtesy of the Hull & Barnsley Railway Stock Fund.

WITHAM'S SIDINGS

The Hull & Barnsley Railway and the Lancashire & Yorkshire Railway granted each other running powers to work goods and mineral trains over each Company's tracks. In the case of the latter the Lancashire & Yorkshire worked into Hull and in return the Hull & Barnsley was able to work to Wakefield. As a result of this working arrangement the Hull & Barnsley introduced a fast goods service to Wakefield. Departing from Spring Bank West at 10.00 p.m., the train would make stops for water at Carlton and Calder Bridge Junction before running into Witham's Sidings, Wakefield, at about 1.00 a.m. Booked to return at 2.30 a.m. the fast goods called at Pontefract and Hensall Junction before arriving back at Spring Bank West at 5.33 a.m.

The 'reception committee' which handled the Hull train on its arrival at Witham's Sidings would be similar to that seen on the day shift. Signalmen, shunting staff and engine crew would all be on hand to smooth the path of the incoming late night fast goods. Interesting yard furniture in this Lancashire & Yorkshire composition, essential in accepting the train, include the siding's large, well kept signal cabin and the yard's shunting engine, an 0-6-0 saddle tank, No.549, originally built as a tender locomotive by Barton Wright and converted into its later configuration by John A.F. Aspinall.

R.I.P.

Queen Victoria reigned on the throne of England longer than any other monarch in English history. When she died in January, 1901, in her sixty-third year of sovereignty, the nation entered a period of deep mourning. The day of the Queen's interment, Saturday the 2nd of February, was decreed by His Majesty, King Edward VII, a day of general mourning. At precisely 2.30 p.m., the hour appointed for the Queen's funeral at Frogmore, Windsor, as a mark of respect all movement throughout the Hull & Barnsley Railway system ceased for a period of ten minutes. Trains were brought to a standstill and servants of the Company on duty were instructd to stand quietly at their posts for the announced period of respect.

Almost identical instructions were issued by the Hull & Barnsley following the death of King Edward VII in 1910.

Reproduction courtesy of Christopher Young.

HULL AND BARNSLEY RAILWAY.

Funeral of Her late Majesty Queen Victoria.

In accordance with the direction of His Majesty the King, Saturday next, the 2nd February, will be observed as a day of General Mourning.

The Offices, Workshops, and Premises of the Company will be closed and business suspended. The Goods and Mineral Train Services will be discontinued, and the Passenger Train Services will run as on Sundays, supplemented as advertised and shewn in the Working Notice.

At the hour appointed for the Funeral at Windsor, viz., 2-30 p.m., a cessation of all movement throughout the Company's system for a period of TEN minutes is ordered. Trains are to be brought to a stand and to remain motionless, and every servant of the Company who is on duty, is to stand quietly in his place for the period named.

WALTER H. WOOD,
General Manager.

GENERAL MANAGER'S OFFICE, HULL,
February 1st, 1901.

'Jubilee' Class 6P 5F, 'Barham', No.45653, is seen at its final resting place, the former Hull & Barnsley Sculcoates goods yard sidings, August 1965. Albert Draper & Son Ltd. scrap metal merchants began to cut up ex-British Railways steam locomotives at their subsidiary yard at Sculcoates from early 1964. The scrapping of locomotives continued apace until the closure of the yard in late 1967. The business was then transferred to the former Hull & Barnsley Neptune Street depot. Bereft of chimney, coupling rods and connecting rods, the former London Midland & Scottish Railway class 4-6-0 locomotive, 'Barham', presents a sorry sight in the days before its eventual demise. Out of a total of 191 named 'Jubilee' class locomotives originally built for the London Midland & Scottish, 'Barham' was one of fourteen members of this fine class successfully tendered for disposal by Draper's. No.45653 eventually succumbed to the cutter's torches in August 1965.
Photograph courtesy of Ted Tuxworth.

In preparation

A companion volume, similar in content, is currently in preparation. A compilation of photographs from the author's collection will feature the Railways of Hull, Yorkshire and Lincolnshire.

Titles by the same author:

'Early Days on the Road':
A photographic record of Hull and the East Riding. Hutton Press, 1987.

'Wings over Yorkshire':
A Pictorial Survey. Pioneer Aviators and their Flying Machines. Hutton Press, 1988.